The Littlest Star

The Littlest Star

The Potter's Quill
The Mimzie Collection

Tamie Burton

The Littlest Star

Text Copyright by Tamie M. Burton

Illustrations Copyright by Tamie M. Burton

All Rights Reserved.

ISBN 9798326569004

Dedicated to
Brittnie, Courtney & Eli
May you never be too old
to feel the magic of Christmas

A billion stars fill the sky
How to find the right one
Searching for something as they fly
The perfect star to get the job done
Three angels hurry along

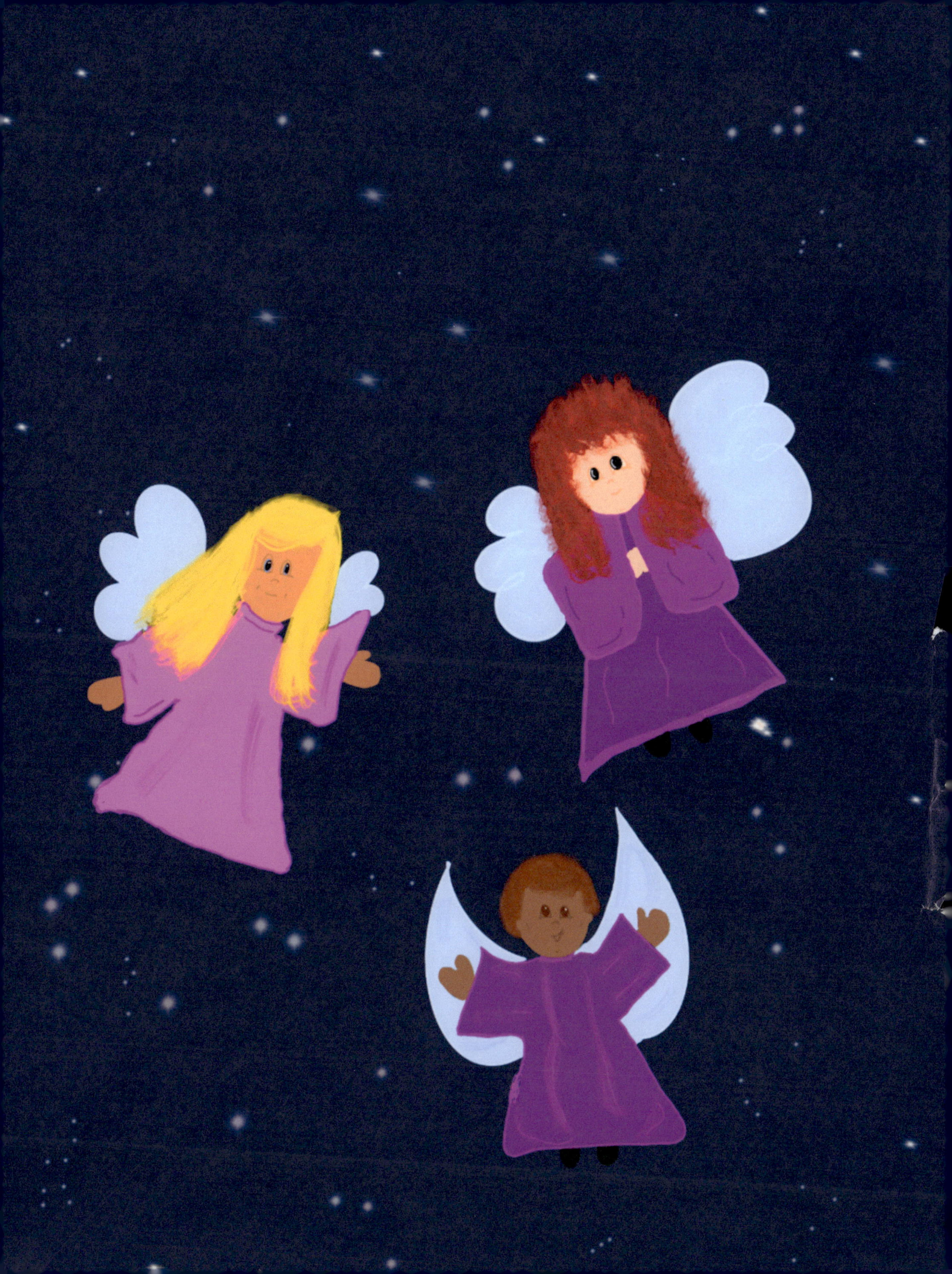

Searching the heavens, high and low
As one angel begins to slow
That one, that one looks strong
But that is just a little star

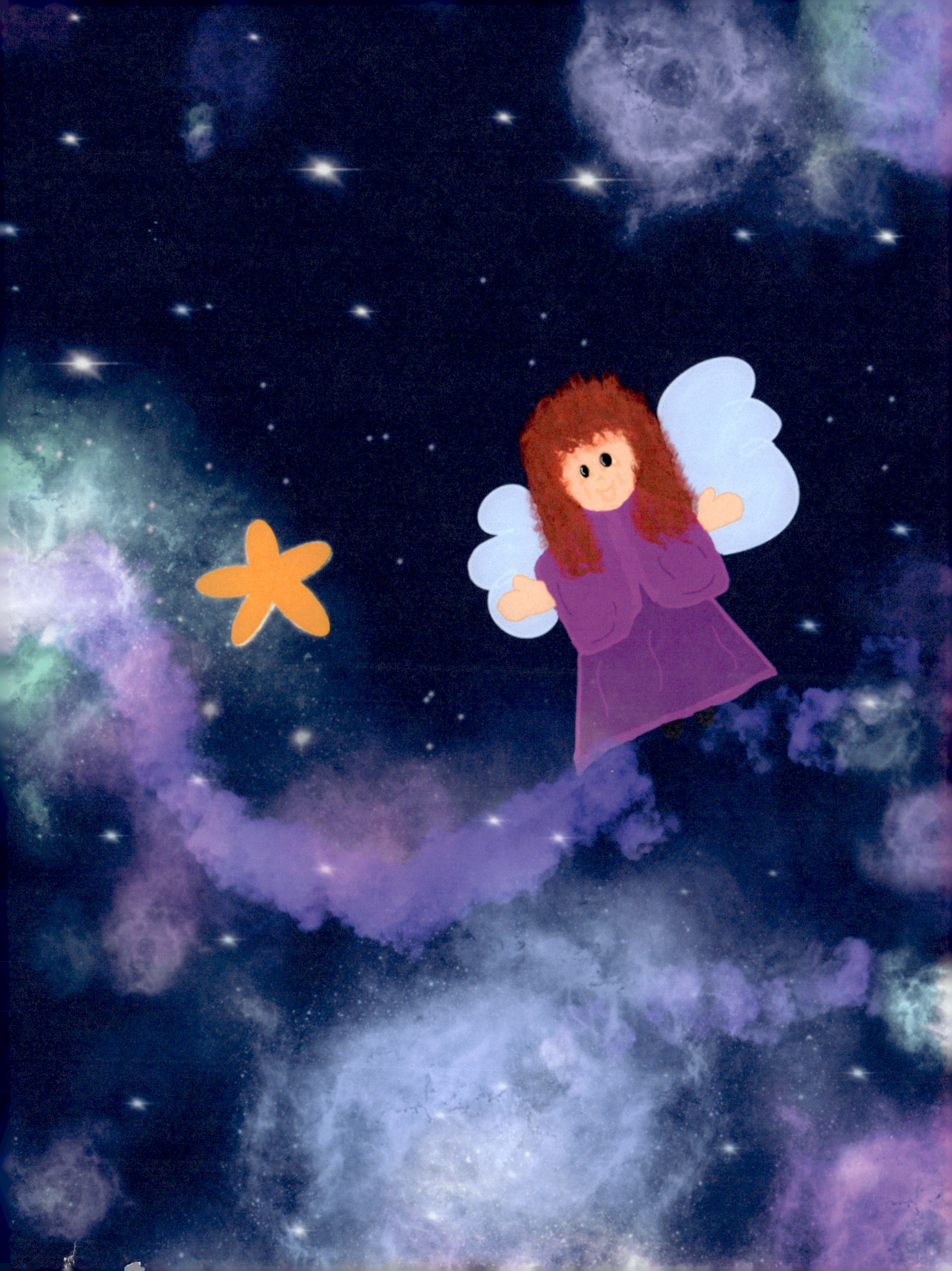

We can sing our song
And tell of the newborn King
The angels surround the little star
And told of the love
the baby would bring
To all the world both near and far
A savior, the song would ring

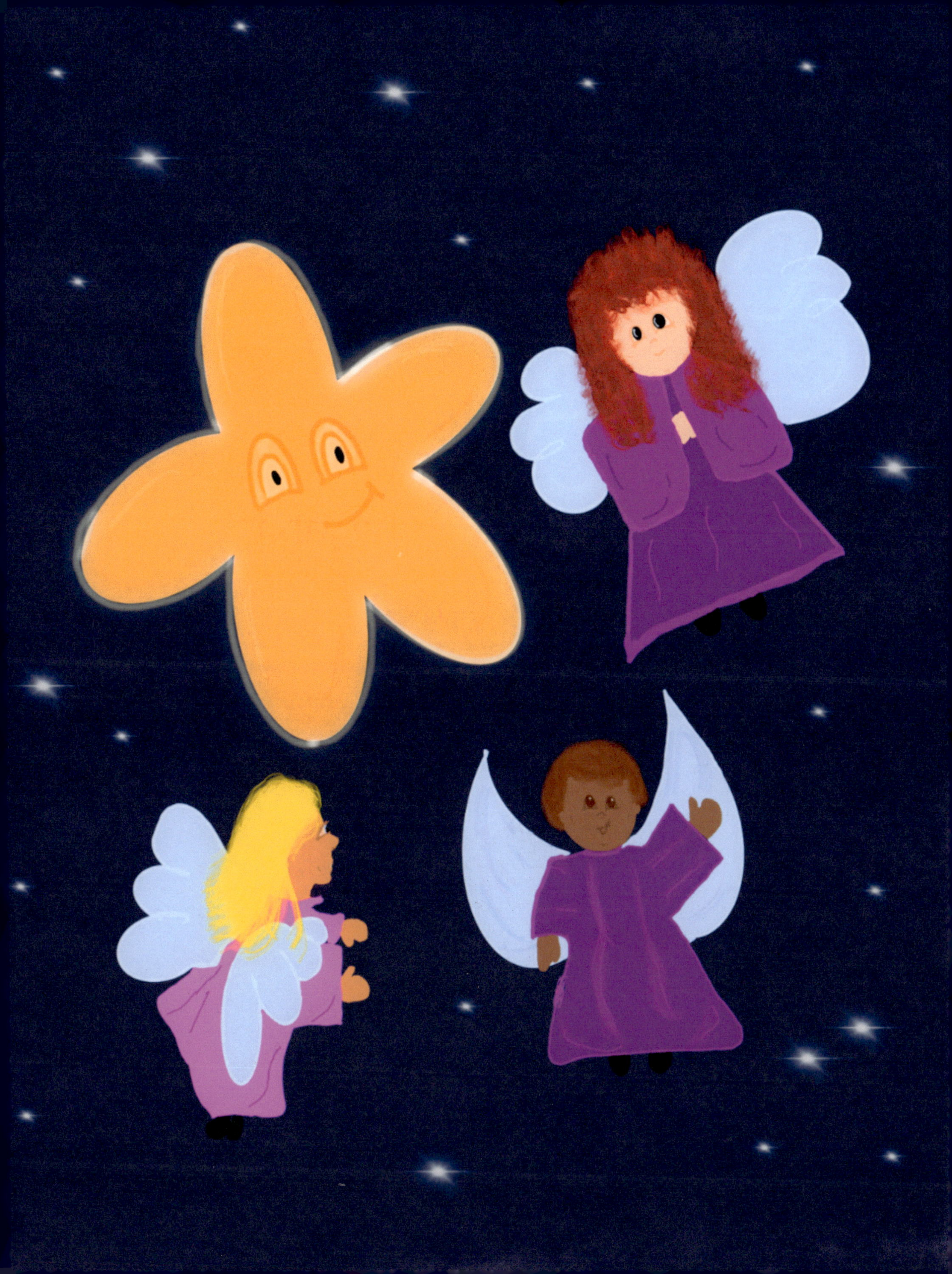

The little star listened close
The heavenly voices began to sing
The story of Hope, Joy,
Love and Peace

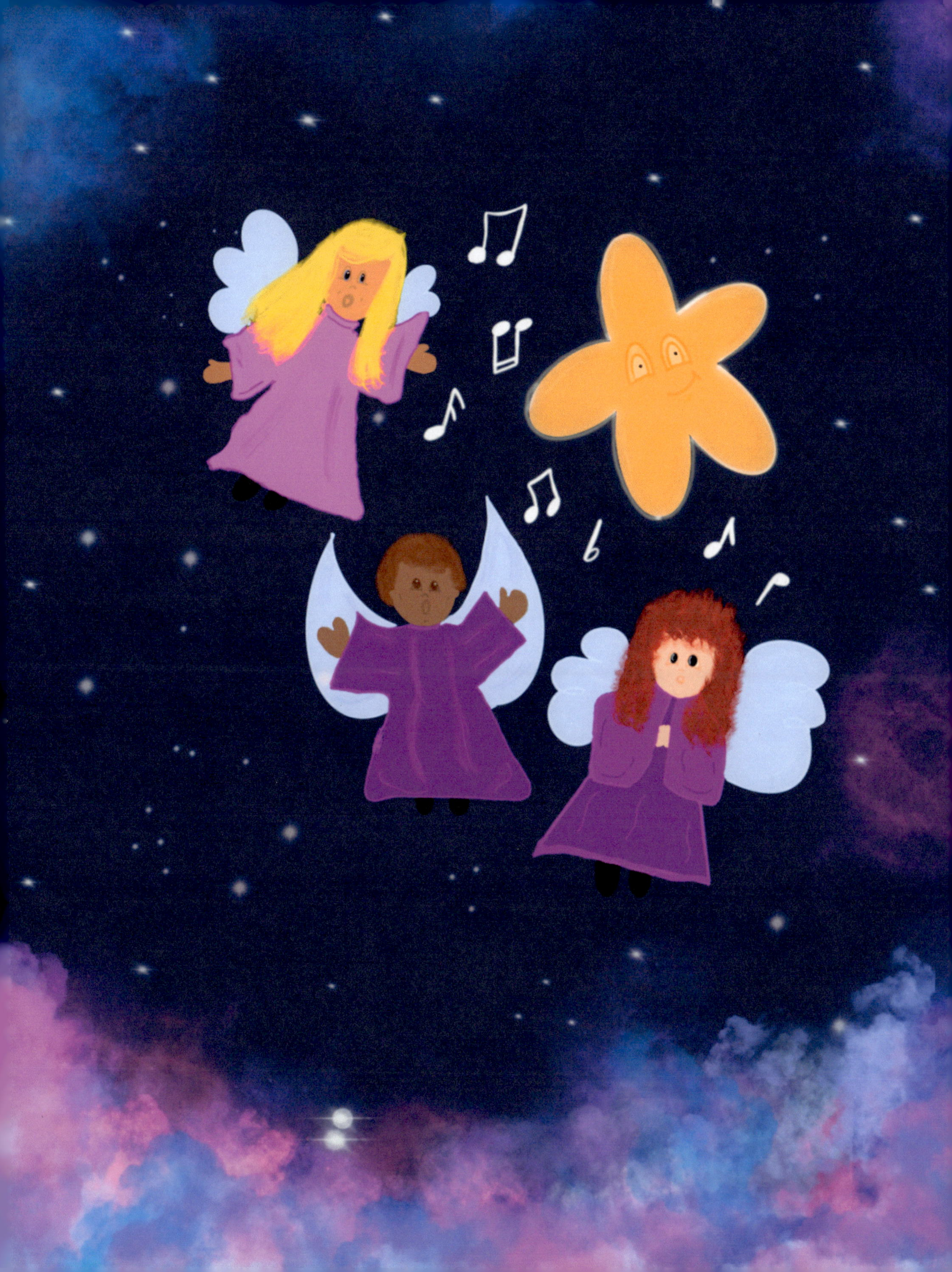

The little star began to grow
The wonder wouldn't cease
Can I see the glorious King?

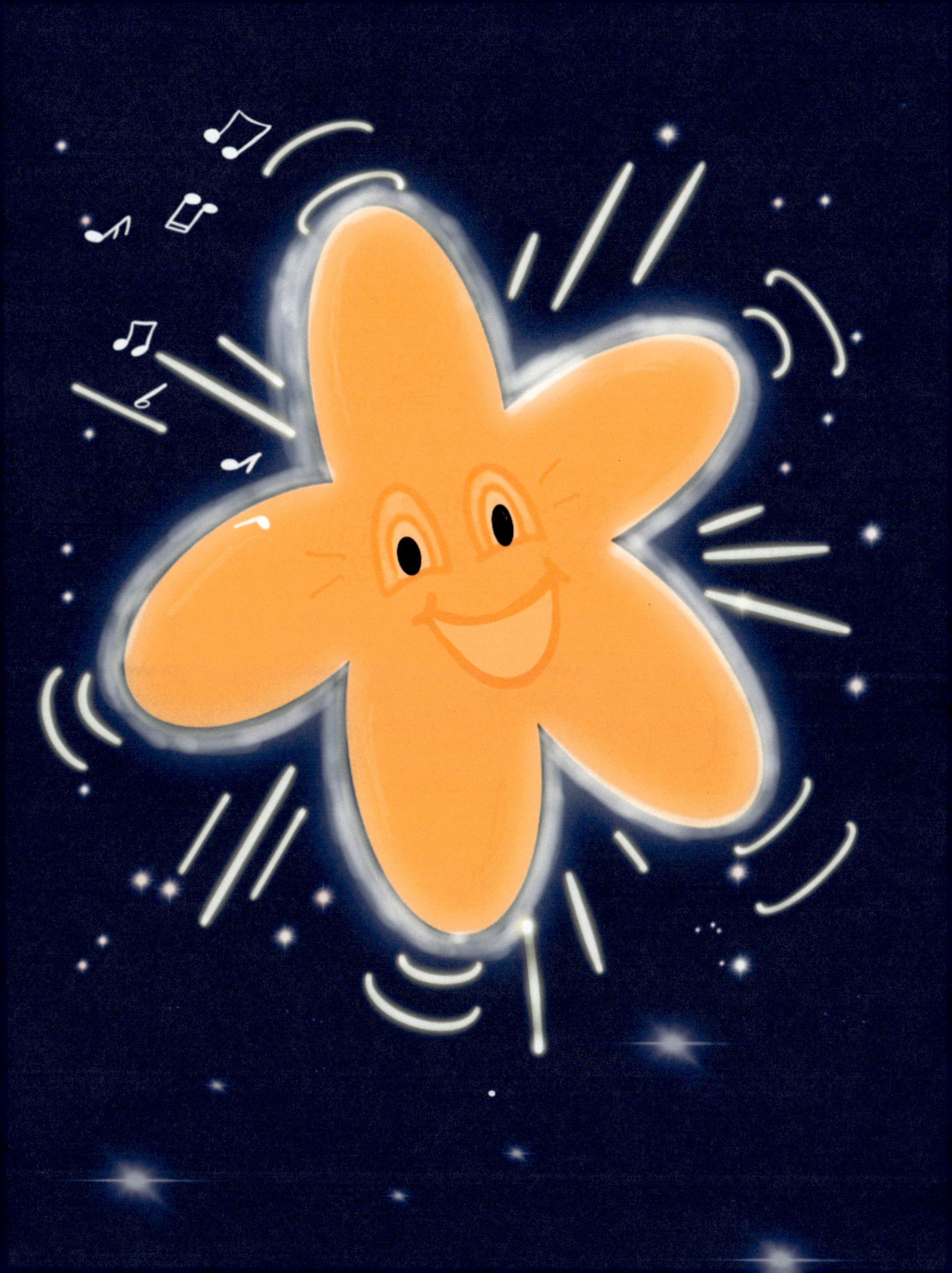

The angels sang,
you can show the world our King
Shine big and bright with all your might
Below, you can light the way

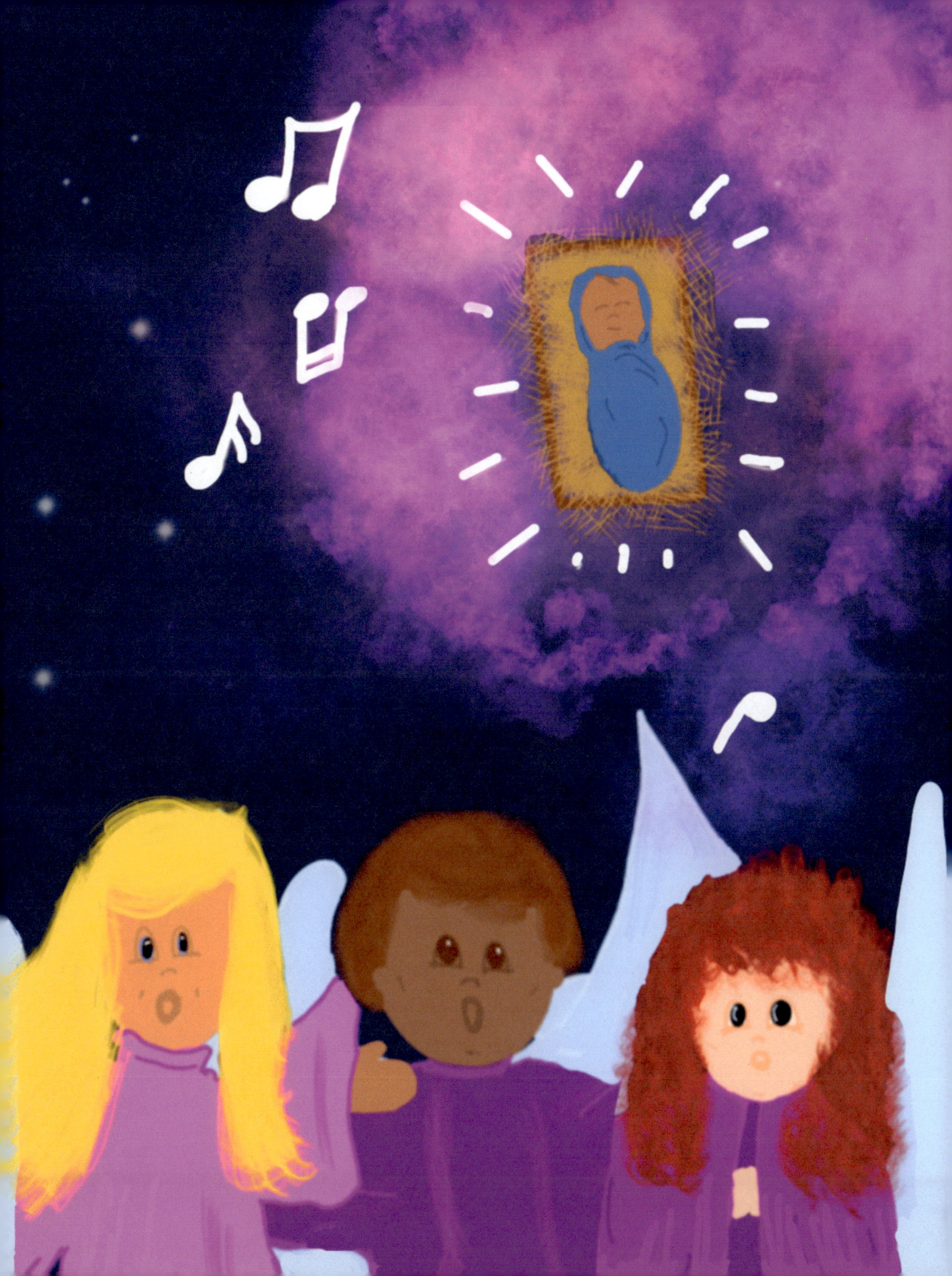

Filled with joy the star became a sight
Over Bethlehem it shown
Showing the world, the humble throne
The star smiled down on the
Holy site
Leading the pilgrimage
through the night

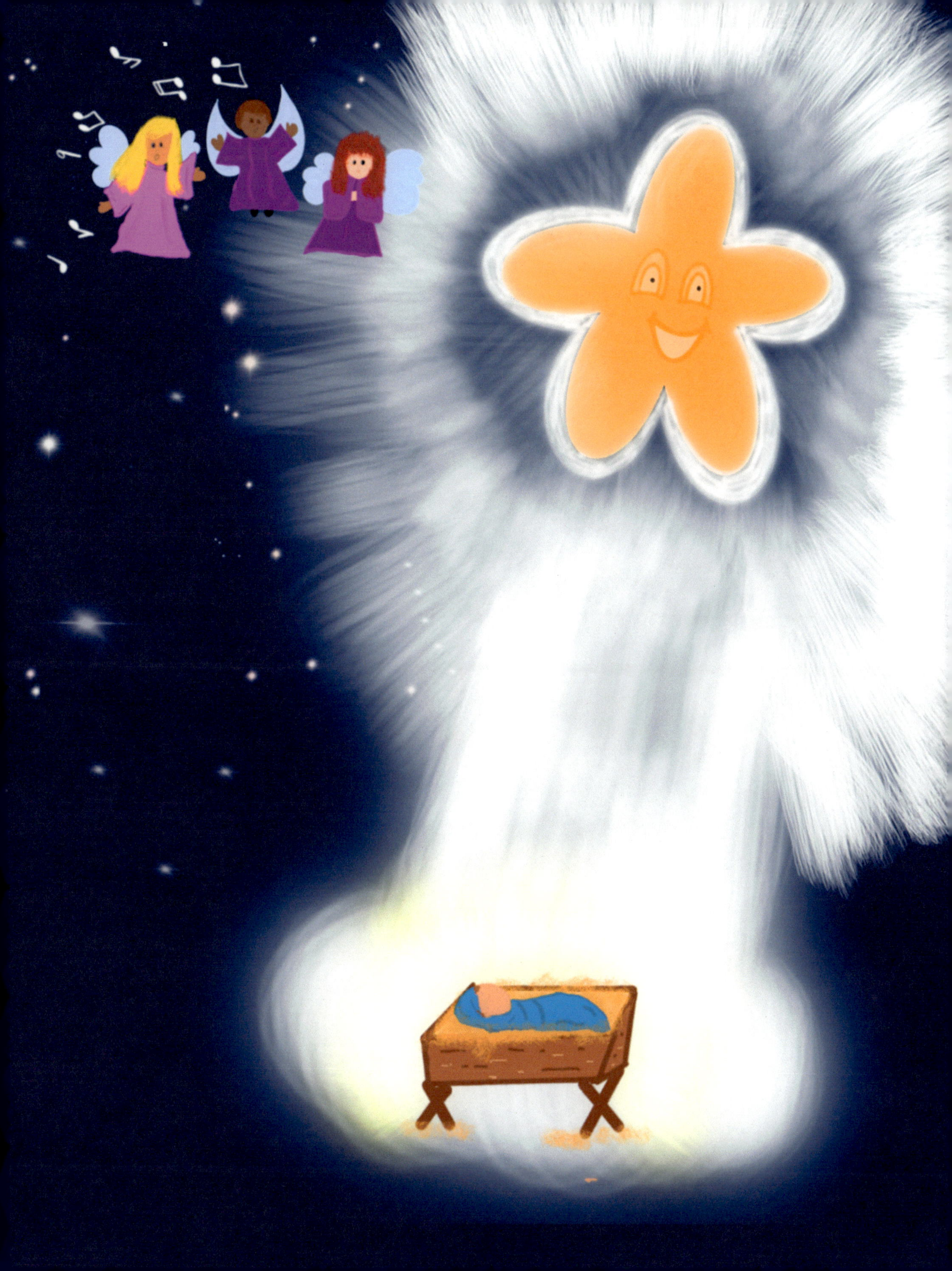

Baby Jesus, they came to see
Bowing down on bended knee
The Messiah seen in the
star's bright light
Oh, what a glorious sight!

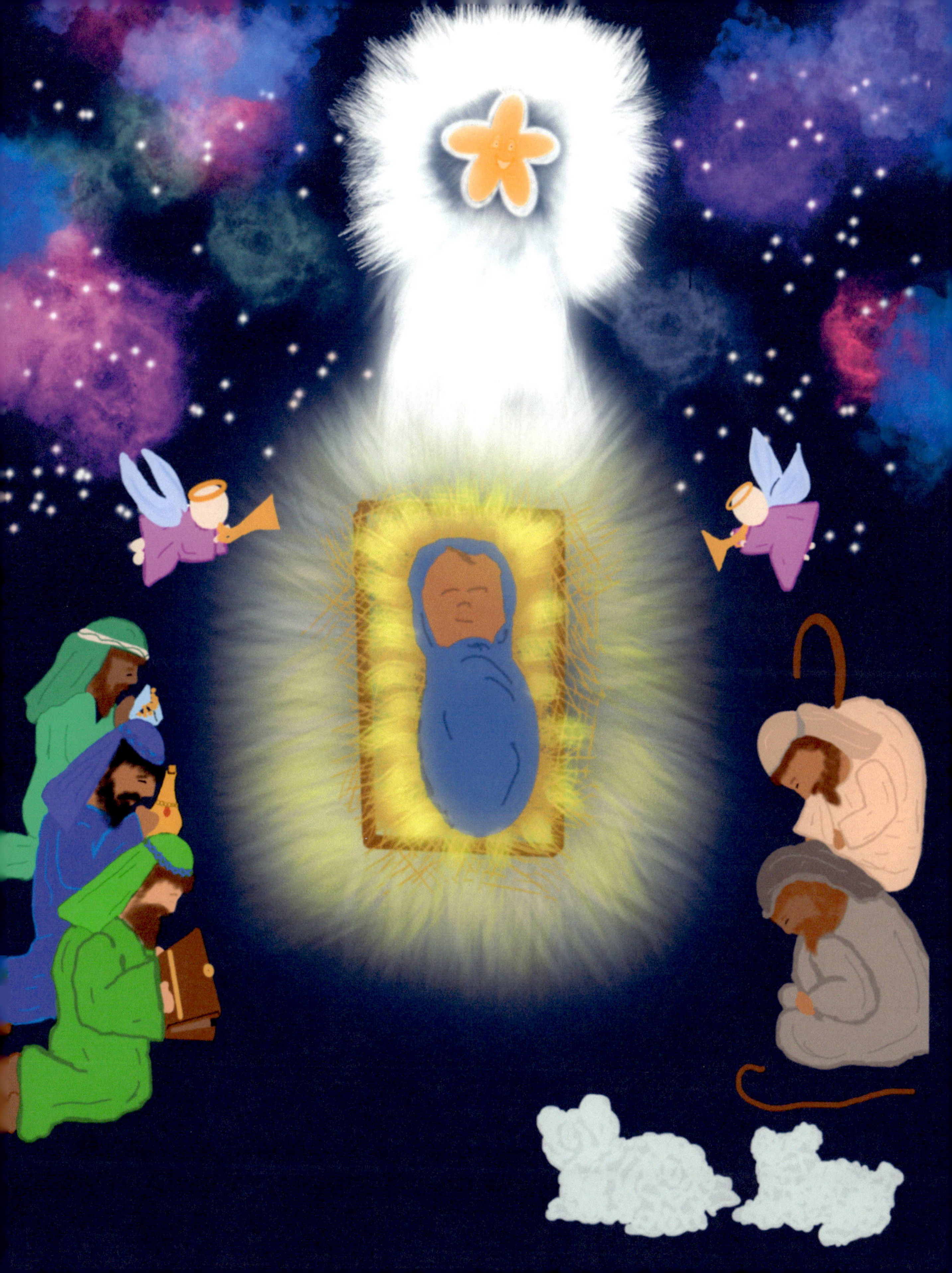

For unto you
was born this day
in the city of David,
a Savior,
who is
Christ the Lord
Luke 2:11 ESV

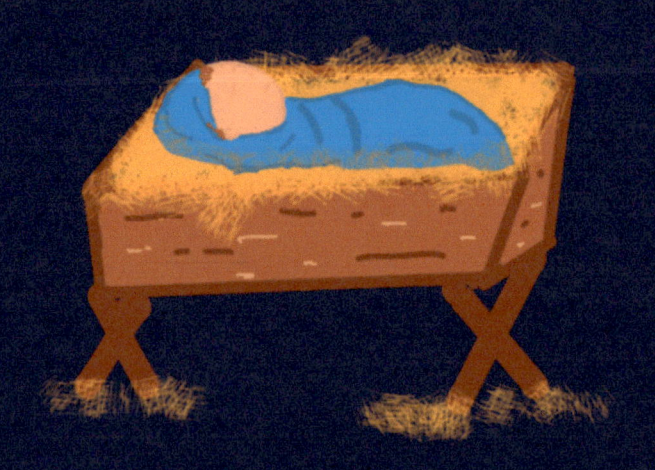

Jesus loves you
Dear little one
Let Him guide you
Along your way
Follow Him
He will not lead you astray
Love everyone with your heart
It is what He wanted from the start
You may stumble, you may fall
But Jesus is with you through it all
Trust in Him
Have faith and know
Oh how much He loves you so

Merry

Christmas

About the Author

Tamie Burton was born and raised in the Mississippi Delta, where the rich heritage of arts is part of every day life. She grew up with a passion for drawing, painting and writing. The inspiration for writing children's books blossomed after her first grandchild was born. Tamie illustrates her stories herself so that her grandchildren will have something special completely from her. Sharing her stories with other children has been a great joy. Tamie also enjoys handbuilding pottery, which is where her business name was born The Potter's Quill.

Enjoy.

Made in the USA
Columbia, SC
03 September 2024